Learning to Read, Step by Step!

Ready to Read   Preschool–Kindergarten
• big type and easy words • rhyme and rhythm • picture clues
For children who know the alphabet and are eager to begin reading.

Reading with Help   Preschool–Grade 1
• basic vocabulary • short sentences • simple stories
For children who recognize familiar words and sound out new words with help.

Reading on Your Own   Grades 1–3
• engaging characters • easy-to-follow plots • popular topics
For children who are ready to read on their own.

Reading Paragraphs   Grades 2–3
• challenging vocabulary • short paragraphs • exciting stories
For newly independent readers who read simple sentences with confidence.

Ready for Chapters   Grades 2–4
• chapters • longer paragraphs • full-color art
For children who want to take the plunge into chapter books but still like colorful pictures.

STEP INTO READING® is designed to give every child a successful reading experience. The grade levels are only guides; children will progress through the steps at their own speed, developing confidence in their reading.

Remember, a lifetime love of reading starts with a single step!

For Clay and Sienna
—S.C.

To my family, for naming me in the memory of
my grandmother Kamala
—K.N.

Text copyright © 2021 by Shasta Clinch
Interior illustrations copyright © 2021 by Kamala Nair

Step into Reading, Random House, and the Random House colophon are registered trademarks of Penguin Random House LLC.

Photograph credits: Cover: Getty Images/Bloomberg; p. 3: Getty Images/Win McNamee for Getty Images News; p. 4: Getty Images/Pool for Getty Images News; p. 29: Getty Images/San Francisco Chronicle/Hearst Newspapers; p. 31: Getty Images/Olivier Douliery for AFP; p. 32: Getty Images/Drew Angerer for Getty Images News

Visit us on the Web!
StepIntoReading.com
rhcbooks.com

Educators and librarians, for a variety of teaching tools, visit us at RHTeachersLibrarians.com

Library of Congress Cataloging-in-Publication Data
Names: Clinch, Shasta, author. | Nair, Kamala M., illustrator.
Title: Kamala is speaking : vice president for the people / by Shasta Clinch ; illustrated by Kamala Nair.
Other titles: Vice president for the people
Description: First edition. | New York : Random House, [2021] | Series: Step into reading, step 2
Summary: "An illustrated biography of Vice President Kamala Harris" —Provided by publisher.
Identifiers: LCCN 2021018769 (print) | LCCN 2021018770 (ebook) |
ISBN 978-0-593-43029-3 (trade) | ISBN 978-0-593-43030-9 (lib. bdg.) |
ISBN 978-0-593-43031-6 (ebook)
Subjects: LCSH: Harris, Kamala, 1964—Juvenile literature. | Vice-presidents—United States—Biography—Juvenile literature. | Women legislators—United States—Biography—Juvenile literature. | African American women legislators—Biography—Juvenile literature. | Legislators—United States—Biography—Juvenile literature.
Classification: LCC E901.1.H37 C55 2021 (print) | LCC E901.1.H37 (ebook) | DDC 973.934092 [B]—dc23

Printed in the United States of America
10 9 8 7 6 5 4 3 2 1
First Edition

STEP INTO READING®

STEP 2 · READING WITH HELP

A BIOGRAPHY READER

KAMALA IS SPEAKING
Vice President for the People

by Shasta Clinch
illustrations by Kamala Nair

Random House 🏠 New York

Kamala Harris is
the first female
vice president of the
United States of America.
She is the first
Black, Indian person
in this role, too.

Kamala knows
other women and
people of color will
follow in her footsteps.

Kamala Devi Harris was born on October 20, 1964, in Oakland, California.

Her mother
was from India.
Her father
was from Jamaica.
Kamala's parents
came to California
to study at a university.

Kamala's parents fought for justice and equal rights.

They felt all people
should be treated fairly.
Kamala went with them
to protests
at a very young age.

Then Kamala's little sister
was born.
Kamala watched over Maya.

That taught her to help and protect someone who needed her.

Kamala rode the bus
to school.
She was among the
first students of color
to go to her school.

There she learned about
lots of people
and cultures.

At church,
Kamala learned about joy,
empathy, and kindness.

At her community center,
she learned about
speaking up for others
from some powerful
women.

MAYA ANGELOU

FREEDOM

When Kamala was twelve,
she and her family
moved to Montreal, Canada.
There was a big lawn
outside their apartment.

KEEP OFF
the GRASS

Kids were not allowed
to play on it!
Kamala and her sister
did not think
that was fair.

They held a protest.

It worked!

The rule was changed.

Kamala thought about
how she could
help others.

Kamala knew
that some people
were treated unfairly.

It was sometimes
because of the color
of their skin.
She wanted to make things
more fair.

Kamala decided
to become a lawyer.
She studied hard
in college
and law school.

She spoke up for others
and marched against
inequality.

At her first court case,
she was introduced as
"Kamala Harris,
for the people."

She wanted to help
even more people.
So Kamala ran for office.

Kamala has held
many elected positions.

She has helped people
finish their education
and get jobs.

She has helped people
keep their homes.

As a senator,
Kamala fought
for women's rights
and to protect
the environment.
She fought for
people who came
to America
from other countries.
She also ran for
president.

Kamala reached
the White House,
but not as president.
Joe Biden chose her
as his vice presidential
running mate.
Together, they won
the 2020 election!

As vice president,
Kamala Harris will keep
speaking up and
fighting for the people!